Take My Wrinkled Hand, Lord

Take My Wrinkled Hand, Lord

"A humorous devotional for the aging"

Anita Nyszik

authorHOUSE®

AuthorHouse™
1663 Liberty Drive
Bloomington, IN 47403
www.authorhouse.com
Phone: 1-800-839-8640

First published by AuthorHouse   09/29/2011

ISBN: 978-1-4634-5018-2 (sc)
ISBN: 978-1-4634-5019-9 (ebk)

Library of Congress Control Number: 2011916610

Printed in the United States of America

Any people depicted in stock imagery provided by Thinkstock are models, and such images are being used for illustrative purposes only. Certain stock imagery © Thinkstock.

This book is printed on acid-free paper.

*A VERY SPECIAL "THANK YOU" TO MY
YOUNGEST DAUGHTER, DONNA TRUINI,
WHO IS VERY COMPUTER KNOWLEDGEABLE
AND SO EAGER TO HELP.*

SHE IS ONE OF MY VERY SPECIAL BLESSINGS.

Contents

❧ Chapter 1

How Empty A Life Is When It Is Surrounded By Only "Things"

The dumpster was being delivered onto the driveway. They ordered the largest one, being sure they were going to need it.

It had been three weeks since their mom, Cassie, had passed away. They really missed her, but now they had the job of selling her home. They had to clean it all out before the real estate agent would put it on the market.

Bill and Joy had been begging Cassie to begin weeding out, especially the last few years, but Cassie saved everything. You could hardly find an empty spot on the sofa to sit down.

They started in the living room, removing everything they could find. It included lots of old newspapers, a package of new socks which disintegrated in their hands when opened, old sweaters with golf ball sized holes in them. One side of the room was strewn with dead pots of flowers, 8 pairs of worn out shoes, 50 paperback books which were probably never read and numerous other paraphernalia which should have hit the garbage can long ago.

Bill and Joy could not believe the amount of junk Cassie had collected. They wondered if she ever threw anything out in all her fifty years she lived in the house. Try as they may, their anger kept building in spite of their love for her.

They still had six more rooms, and some were in worse condition then the living room. The dumpster was half full already. They realized this weeding out was going to take them weeks!

Looking at each other in amazement, they both realized (almost at the same time) that the garage was almost filled to it's brim. They both felt the need to scream.

Don't let the people you leave behind suffer with all your "stuff". They want to remember you as the kind, loving person they loved and not the world's worst junk collector.

Sometimes I go from room to room looking at my treasures. At least I think they're treasures, but when "God" takes me home and the kids have to clean this place, I hope they consider them treasures and not just mom's old junk.

"Life is so much more than the things we store"

§

True contentment is not in having everything, but in being satisfied with everything you have.

§

God smiles when we say "Thank you, Father," and not, "Give me more".

§

Somehow, as we age, material things seem so much less important.

- Family and friends are important.
- A good nights sleep is important.
- Having a extra tube of Bengay (just in case) is important.

When we recall our past, we usually remember that the simple things in life were the things that gave us the most pleasure.

§

If our fulfillment depends on material possessions, we are crushed when we lose them, but if our joy is found in the "Lord", nothing can disrupt it.

§

Silver and gold could not redeem our souls. "Jesus" took care of that on the cross.

§

The three immutable facts:

- You own things.
- You will eventually pass away.
- Someone will get those things.

Or

- They will end up in the town dump.

"Lord", I need to realize that as I get older, I really need to simplify a little bit to be more comfortable.
    Like:

Having enough to eat
Having clean clothes to wear
Having a warm comfy house
And a comfy reclining chair
A bed, a lamp, a book or two
A, thankful heart in prayer to you
My needs and wants are but a few
A little, "Lord", will more than do.

A LITTLE'S BOYS SMILE

Jenny was so thankful for her neighbors visit especially when she brought her little son, Billy with her. He was always so excited when he played with her late husband's collection of "Hess" trucks. He would play with them for hours while Jenny and Billy's mom visited together.

Today, when they went to leave, Jenny told him to pick two of the trucks to take home. How she wished her late husband could see the smile on Billy's face. Just material things, but they made a little boy so happy.

MY WORLD OF MINIATURES

I have always loved the world of miniatures. Tiny chairs, tiny teddy bears, tiny little furniture. I have shelves of it, and it all has to be dusted.

Today as I sat in contemplation of hours of dusting, I thought to myself, "do I really need all this stuff?" and I answered myself back. "You certainly don't" (at this stage of the game, we can even talk to ourselves and no one even notices)

"Lord", I ask one thing of thee, the gift of true simplicity"

Let your conversation be without covetousness; and be content with such things as ye have. For "He" has said "I will never leave thee nor forsake thee." (Hebrews 13:5)

"GOD HAS A TIME FOR EVERYTHING"

Usually, in everyone's life, there is a very special place he or she just loves to be. For me, it is my little camper in the woods. I have had this little bit of heaven for nine years now.

It is 26 feet long, with a large wooden porch on it. I have spent such wonderful weekends there. The smell of pine and burning campfires still invigorate me. This has been my own "special place."

I pull into my campsite, open my door, make a huge pot of coffee and sit down to write and read to my hearts content.

Unfortunately, the elements of such terribly cold winters always take a toll on all our campers, high winds bring branches down through roofs; dampness sneaks in and does its own fair share of damage. My little bit of heaven" always needs lots of tender loving care, but it is a labor of love for me.

Lately, arthritis has taken its toll. I can no longer pull myself up off the ladder and onto the roof to check for any damage.

I also find it extremely difficult to reach up and wash off the green moss which always collects on the outside of the camper body. My hands have lost some of their strength, my wrists have weakened too!

My three children have always offered to come and help, but their lives are busy enough. I feel it just isn't fair to trouble them with something I, myself, should be able to do.

In Ecclesiastes, "God" tells us that there is a time for everything. I know "He" is telling me that my time to sell this precious place has finally come.

So I cried a bit and then I put up my sign and then I cried a little more. Just seeing that sign out front broke my heart, but "God" knows what we need before we even ask.

My youngest daughter has just told us we are going to have a grandchild! Another of my dreams is being realized. My joy is totally overwhelming!

It will be much easier to leave my little piece of heaven to open my heart for this precious little miracle "God" is sending us. I won't even feel old when he calls me "grandma".

I will pray that whoever the lucky people are that buy my camper, will treasure it as much as I have.

The man who frees himself of all unnecessary possessions truly does possess all things.

§

Love people, not things
Use things, not people.

§

Our most important possessions are our memories. In nothing else are we rich, in nothing else are we poor.

§

In regard to collecting things you'll never see a U-haul trailer behind a hearse.

LET US LEARN TO LAUGH AT OURSELVES WHEN:

We make an apple pie and forget to put the cinnamon in.

§

We get in bed at night and its cozy and it's warm . . . . because we forgot to turn off the electric blanket that morning.

§

We forgot to check the toilet paper before we sat down . . . ugh!

§

Worry is like a rocking chair, it gives you something to do, but gets you nowhere.

Chapter 2

"Lord, Make Me A Nicer Me"

Be the first to say hello.

Bend a little, you're not always right!

Return all things you borrow.

Admit your mistakes.

Avoid negative people.

Be kinder than necessary.

Smile a lot. It costs nothing and is beyond price.

Self pity dries up sympathy with others.

Share each others problems.

When meeting others, let me be the first to smile.

You are never fully dressed until you wear a smile.

Smiles never go up in price or down in value.

When I start to find fault with all I see. It's time to start looking for what's wrong with me.

A person wrapped up in himself makes a very small package.

It isn't your position that makes you happy or unhappy, it's your disposition.

Never interrupt anyone . . . ever!

Don't use time or words carelessly. Neither can be retrieved.

Show respect for all living things.

Never tell others they look tired or depressed.

Always criticize in private.

Leave everything a little better than you found it.

Put a shocking pink tennis ball on your car antenna. You'll find your car every time. I do!

If you are able, volunteer in a hospital or somewhere else just to keep your mind alert and stable.

MY PRECIOUS KATHERINE

I spent a number of years as a health aide going from home to home serving up huge doses of caring, cleaning, sensitivity, and hours of bathing, but the biggest dose of what these aged people need is lots and lots of love.

Extra things like soaking their feet in warm water (they love it) or rubbing their arms and legs with aspercreme took more time than I was allowed but how these people need those extra minutes you give them.

There are so many different kinds of aides, there are aides that glance around the scene and evaluate what needs to be done for patient and home and go about making a patients home comfortable for him or her. "God" bless these people for they do their very best.

There are also aides that are over and abundantly lazy. They will come in, take off their coat, and sit with the patient, doing nothing but talk. It doesn't matter if the patient hasn't had her breakfast and has no idea where lunch is coming from. The aide carefully watches the time and is out in a flash.

One little lady I worked with was 98 years young. A hairdresser had come to her home to wash and perm her hair. This woman let Katherine fall backward after washing her hair and Katherine struck her head on the porcelain sink. She was never strong after this.

Her legs hurt her, but she always had a smile for me. She appreciated everything I did for her. She was so full of gratitude. We went through numerous tubes of aspercreme. It helped.

She was a woman of faith. She would get up very early and pray for her whole family and even me. She never complained even though I knew she was in pain.

She once told me that since her husband passed away, "Jesus" had become her true love. She would talk about her dying like it was to be a huge celebration. She knew where she was going, and she was ready. I loved her dearly. Everyone loved her. She was special!

Katherine got her wish. She is now walking with her great love and I am sure she needs no more aspercreme. One of Katherine's favorite sayings was "We all have clouds in our lives" Clouds will pass" . . . I miss you Katherine!

"HE" KNOWS WHAT WE NEED

She pulled up the blinds and started washing them, she couldn't believe how black the paper towel was. It had been a while since they had been washed.

Her family would be doing all the cooking, but they would be having Thanksgiving at her house. Everyone was coming, and she was thrilled. Bootsie, (that's what they called her) didn't get company very often these days.

She would make her popular big bowl of rice pudding. She would set the table elegantly with her beautiful china, and when the meal was over, she would give the set to her only daughter. She had set her eyes on it long ago. She had already given her son's wife the lovely Christmas china that she loved.

Her home was cozy. She was always thankful for what she was able to do.

As she prayed before going to bed (she used to kneel beside the bed, but lately her knees couldn't take the pain, so now she said her prayers in bed). She knew "Jesus" didn't care where she said them. She closed by asking "Him" to give her the strength to vacumn the rugs and mop the floor.

The doorbell rang the next afternoon. It was her neighbor. She explained that her daughter's school was planning a field trip and the students needed to work and earn their money themselves.

This was an answer to prayer, Tina would be able to vacumn the rugs and wash the floor for her. She asked Tina if $10.00 would be enough. Tina was thrilled. It was her first job.

That night Bootsie expressed her thanks in her prayers. "Jesus" had never failed her. She knew without a doubt that "He" could be trusted.
She trusted "Him" all the time.

§

Middle age is the time when a narrow waist and a broad mind change places.

LAUGHTER MAKES THE HEART CHEERFUL

When I was 27 I felt like a pebble on the beach. Now I feel like the whole beach

§

I may be an antique, but aren't antiques valuable?

§

When grandmothers of today hear that word "Chippendales" they don't think of chairs.

§

If God had to give a woman wrinkles, he should have put them on the souls of her feet.

§

Middle age is when you're sitting home on Saturday night and the telephone rings, and you hope it's not for you.

❧ *Chapter 3*

Jewelry Takes Peoples Mind Off Your Wrinkles (Accepting Change)

Once a day is gone, it can never be recaptured. Our lives change and we must learn to change with them. "God" helps us to prepare for different stages of our maturity.

We can all expect change. An optimistic attitude toward the future is the secret of dealing with change. Living long and loving it is what change is all about.

Life boasts few things that you can depend on, but change is one of them. We fear the loss of agility the most. The gaining of a new wrinkle every morning does not come easy.

The transition from mid-life to retirement is easy for some, and boring for others. It means not having to get up every morning, not having to be on a schedule. It means being able to catch our breath and live at a more amiable pace.

How terrific it is to be able to relax in the afternoon in your recliner with the dog or cat on your lap. No one is going to catch you and say "I wish that was all

I had to do". No one is going to make you feel guilty. You can relax as long as you like. You realize that your days will be so much more comfortable without that "always having to be doing something" feeling.

I think we have to realize that we can't stop the wind from blowing, but we can ask the "Lord" to teach us how to bend. Some changes are actually to our advantage.

TO FACE LIFE'S CHANGES, LOOK TO OUR UNCHANGING "GOD"

It's a sign of aging to admit that we look forward to a slower pace. I want to slow down enough to notice the budding of each new rose, the black velvet looking squirrels that have recently come to our neighborhood. And . . . I want to be quiet enough to hear "His" voice. How often I have whispered a prayer for "Him" to make me slow down enough so that I might not miss all the beauty "He" has given me to see.

Genuine contentment isn't learned all at once. But it always includes being thankful for whatever blessings we have.

"Christ" does not promise to remove all our problems, but "He" does promise to be there with us to help us through them.

Aging is "God's" idea. It's one of the ways "He" keeps us headed homeward. We can't change the process, but we can change our attitude. The mark of true wisdom is the art of knowing how to grow older gently and gracefully.

There are definitely advantages in growing older:

- The turbulence you felt in youth is gone.
- No need, with maturity, to explain yourself. You are accepted for what you are.
- An evening at home is so much more precious than a night of frivolity.
- We live more in the present then in the future.
- We have the time to see the beauty in familiar things, the outstretched arms of a grandchild, the faithfulness of the pets we love and who love us back. The different colors of the sunsets and the backyard robin teaching her babies to fly.

GROWING OLDER IS REALLY KIND OF A LUXURY!

Time is actually a gift from "God", a precious package of life sent to us by our "heavenly father". Time to think, to reflect, to love, laugh, and listen to music and to the ones we love and time to get our spiritual lives in order.

THE SHIPWORM

There is a type of marine clam called a shipworm. It will burrow into wooden ships causing untold damage to them. Little by little, the shipworm destroys the ship. This is what happens to us when we allow ourselves that destroying sense of self pity. Little by little it will destroy us until we are no longer ourselves, until we are someone no one wants to be around.

§

A happy heart makes the face cheerful.
(Proverbs 15:13)

§

When your world is falling apart, trust "Jesus" to hold it together.

§

We must learn to laugh at our limitations as we begin to age:

- Those noisy crackling knee joints
- That extra weight around the middle (we call that middle age)
- Even birthdays . . . . don't think of yourself as growing older, you have now reached the age of silver in your hair, gold in your teeth and lots of lead in your bottom!
- Wrinkles appear where smiles have been.

Wrinkles don't matter to "God". Man looks at the outward appearance, but "God" looks at the heart. (Samuel 16:7)

§

Just a thought—Wrinkles are hereditary. Parents get them from their children.

§

Old age is like a bank account, you withdraw from it what you put in.

§

All that you have, "He" so graciously gives, so thank "Him" and praise "Him" each day that you live.

§

HAPPINESS

A little place to call my own
A comfy worn in chair
A pot of tea singing on the stove
A friend to come and share
My "Lord" to fill my empty times
I feel so happy there

"OUR GOLDEN YEARS"

How often I've heard of the golden years
When life should be easy dispelling our fears
When life demands a much slower pace
Not caring about that new wrinkle on your face
Watching years go by, wondering where they went
Looking at pictures of memories well spent
The children come by, though they live far away
I wait for each visit counting each day
They love me, I know, and they really do care
I smile and I thank them for visits so rare
Their love lingers on even though we're apart
For they all hold a special place in my heart
I know in my heart that I'm never alone
For "Jesus" is with me, my heart is "His" home

Changes come whether we are ready for them or not. Even the cells in our bodies are always in the process of changing, "Jesus" tells us. "I am the "Lord", I do not change". (Malachi 3:6)

§

"Jesus Christ" is the same yesterday, today and forever!

§

Sometimes our problems overwhelm us, but then we go out to our garden and we see the crumbly dirt where the flower is trying to push its way into the world.

Seeing this tells me that life is kind of like a flower. It has to push its way through so much soil to bloom. Is this how your life has been? You can still bloom right where you are.

§

The brook would lose its song if you remove the rocks and stones.

§

There can be no peaks without valleys
There can be no roses without thorns

GOD HAS GIVEN US YET MORE TIME TO:

- Forgive someone
- Tell someone we love them
- Teach our grandchildren true values
- Keep in touch with our friends
- Give someone your best recipes
- Send notes of thanks to loved ones
- De-clutter for everyone's sake

Even when I'm old and grey, do not leave me "Lord". (Psalm 71)

And I say: "I am not worried, "Lord", for your promises are pure Gold.

To be sure, the "golden years" are not always "golden", but it helps to know who to go to when things get rough. The bible tell us: "He" will hide me in the shadow of "His" wings.

IT HELPS WHEN WE CAN LAUGH AT OURSELVES

Three of my friends and I went out to lunch one afternoon. As we sat in the booth together, every few minutes one of them would giggle. I thought nothing of it until I went to the ladies room. When I went to wash my hands, I caught a glimpse of myself in the mirror. I knew why they were laughing. I had put two different earrings on and they didn't even resemble each other. I went back to the table and we had a good laugh. Laughing is like therapy.

Our humanness allows us all to experience limitations. How do we deal with them? Maybe our curtains need washing every eight months instead of every three months. So there is a little dust on the coffee table, not a problem. The pets are fed, the plants are watered, you brushed out the toilet, there's plenty of soup in the pantry, and so you are in better shape than you thought . . . . so relax and let "God"!

§

Sometimes we can substitute something to make ourselves feel better, like a truly gaudy necklace and earring set to take someone's mind off your wrinkles. The gaudier the better I say.

What we "do" can never substitute who we are on the inside in the "secret places" that only "God" can see.

"The older the violin, the sweeter the music.
C. Putnam

§

Some people call our senior citizens "Determined" and some call them "Gutsy".

§

"God" is greater than our weaknesses. When we are weak, "He" is strong.

§

Do not cast me away when I am old; do not forsake me when my strength is gone.
    (Psalm 71:19)

How different would today be if you knew it would be your last one on earth before meeting "God" face to face? We should strive to live every day as if it were our last, for one day it will be.
"Billy Graham"

ON THE DOCK

I read a beautiful story about an old man sitting with his grandson on a dock. It was late afternoon, and they were hoping to catch some "Big Ones" for supper.

They talked about so many things. Why the water looks blue, why there are so many colors in a sunset, the different kinds of fish. Finally, the boy looked up at his grandpa and asked, "does anybody ever see "God"? Son, said his grandpa, lately it's getting so I hardly see anything else.

When the train goes through the tunnel, and everything gets dark, do you jump out of the train? Of course not, you just sit still and trust the engineer to get you through. Don't give up. Just be patient and remind yourself that "God" is still in control!

§

In bringing out the shortness of life, the bible uses many different kinds of illustrations:

A flower, it is lovely, but its beauty is so brief.

Grass is green the first day, but brown and burnt the next.

Wind—passes by and is gone.

In other words, wherever you are . . ."Bloom where you are planted:

§

Using your days wisely can make an eternal difference.

To idle away our last years is to rob ourselves of what could be the best years of our lives. There are still victories to be won, things to do, people to love.

§

The longer we live, the more we know
Old age is the time for wisdom to show

§

A cheerful heart is good medicine, but a broken spirit saps a person's strength. (Proverbs 17:22)

§

My body will change and I'll get older, but I will never lose life's zest because the roads last turn will be the best. "Henry Van Dy"

§

When we're going through a storm, it's easy to feel sorry for ourselves. Sometimes when we focus on others, we can leave our pity party. Feeling sorry for ourselves is the devils favorite tool planned to depress you.

We cannot change yesterday
That is quite clear
Nor start our tomorrows
Until they are here
But this is something
We surely can do
Grow close to "God"
And "He'll" grow closer to you!

MEMORY? NEED A LITTLE HELP?

No one knows better than I do that my memory is not what it used to be. It started with little things like forgetting a name or a well-known telephone number. Then it graduated to my forgetting some ages (even of my children) I knew I was in trouble. I was not used to hurting anyone.

I spoke to God about it, but I didn't get an immediate answer. However, as I cleaned out my junk drawer in the kitchen, I came upon the Post-it note pad my daughter had given me just the week before.

Actually, "God" did give me my answer. Notes . . . I would put them on the refrigerator. Notes for my daughter who does my shopping. Notes to remember to send a card to a sick friend, notes on this month's birthdays, notes to feed the animals. Just kidding, they won't let me forget to feed them.

Thanks "Lord" for post-it notes. I think I'll mention them to a few of my friends. They forget too. So . . . . I wrote a note to call them and put it on the phone. And . . . I write a note to my daughter to buy some extra "notes".

WE LEARN TO LAUGH AT OURSELVES WHEN:

We add some interesting new items to our home, like a high toilet seat, bars to help me get into the tub. I know I need these things, but I'd rather have a hot tub!

§

Our favorite saying amongst our friends is, "I think I'm losing it". But the funny thing is, we know we are.

§

I wish I had a dime for as many times as I've gone into a room and couldn't remember what I came in for. Oh well, it'll come to me sooner or later. Hmmm now I remember, it was to change the cats litter box. Ha!

§

Senior moments are guaranteed to keep us humble.

And "God" Loves humility.

"STAYING YOUNG"

You can continue to stay young as long as you choose to keep a positive attitude.

§

Commit yourself to projects that are a challenge.

§

Read as often as you can. This will keep your mind stimulated and keep you improving yourself.

§

With "Christ", positive emotions replace negative emotions. Weights become wings!

§

Life is never boring to the exploring mind.

§

Seek out friends, literature, books, TV programs, and movies that will amuse, uplift, inspire, motivate and challenge you to be a more interesting as well as a more productive person.

If "God" doesn't remove a problem, "He'll" help you find a way around it.

§

Your posture and your walk more than anything, makes you look young or old.

§

"Jesus" said: "Even when you're old, I will be the same.

§

"God" tells us:
Even when your hair has turned grey, I will take care of you. I made you and I will take care of you. I will carry you and save you.
(Isaiah 46:4)

"LAUGHING IS LIKE THERAPY"

I have everything now that I had twenty years ago,
except now it's all lower.

§

You know you're getting "up there" when the candles
cost more than the cake.
"Bob Hope"

§

We all live with changes:
>   The face has shifted
>   Your hair is thinning
>   Whatever was once standing up
>   Is now laying down

§

It's not usually the big mountain in our paths that make
life hard; it's the small pebbles in our shoes.

§

Count that day lost in which you have not tried to do
something for someone else.

Chapter 4

Love Never Gets Old

No one will remember us for our wrinkles or laugh lines, but they will remember us for our kindnesses, the gentle way we treated them or the love we showed them.

LOVE WAGGED IT'S TAIL

He was truly a human derelict. He was dressed in a dirty, shapeless coat; his hat was battered and stained. He hardly seemed human (or so I thought)

I stood back as he opened a broken gate to a cluttered yard surrounding an unpainted shack.

Suddenly, a small spotted dog ran out to him wagging his tail and jumping up so the man could pet him. I could tell the dog loved this man a great deal.

I watched the two of them walk toward the shack. The dog was totally happy to be with the man.

I was so ashamed. I, who tried to follow the example of "Jesus" and was to love everyone, had judged the man to be only a ruin.

A little dog that had no understanding of "God's" word accepted and loved this man just as he was.

§

If we are compassionate to everyone we encounter, we can reach out to others. "Jesus" tells us to "Love one another"!

LOVE IS BEAUTIFUL!
AND
PEOPLE LOVE TO BE AROUND LOVING
PEOPLE.

OPPORTUNITIES TO BE KIND ARE EASY TO FIND

My friend had a pile of freshly-mended clothes on the front seat of her car. I noticed that the buttons had been sewed on with mismatched threads, and hems were repaired with uneven stitches. "Who on earth repaired these clothes" I asked. My friend laughed out loud "My neighbor" I said. She's 85 years old. She lives alone and this fills up her days. Sometimes she gets lonely. "But you're a terrific seamstress, you could do a much better job yourself" She said. Oh, I'm sure, but my neighbor needs to be needed much more than these clothes need to be perfect.

§

A Friend loveth at all times. (Proverbs 17:17)

§

If you want to be loved, you must love and be loveable. (Ben Franklin)

§

Speak the truth in love. An honest answer is a sign of true friendship.

§

Words can't break bones
But . . . . they can break hearts.

ONE MORE BOUQUET

Our girl scouts marched into the nursing home with piles of beautifully-made colorful flower bouquets. The girls had been instructed to smile and scatter into all the rooms handing out the colorful bouquets.

As the girls gathered to leave the building, I noticed a wheelchair in a corner of the hall. Huddled in it, was a woman with terribly twisted fingers and crooked twisted feet. She smiled at the girls. I told her I was sorry the flowers were all gone. She nodded that she understood. We hurried the girls back to the church.

As I left the church for home, my eyes fell on one last colorful bouquet left under a chair.

I really didn't want to go back to deliver it, but I knew I had to. I returned to the nursing home. The woman was still sitting in the wheelchair in the corner. Her eyes turned misty. "Bless you, oh bless you."

I watched as she desperately tried to tighten her bent fingers around the stems. My heart too, was filled with love, right to the brim!

We can bind up the wounds of the broken hearted with a tiny bit of attention.

§

A big part of "loving" is "listening".

§

Let everything you do be done with love.
(1 Corinthians 16:14)

§

A life lived to help others is the only one that matters.
This is our highest and best use as a person.

SOMETIMES IT HURTS TO BE LOVING

My daughter was angry with me. I've never seen you do anything so cruel before, these little birds have worked so hard building their nest.

I hit the mud shell with my broom again. The last bit of it fell and shattered on the porch

Those robins cannot build their nest and raise their babies here I reminded her. Six cats lounge on this porch all summer. They will eat all the nestlings.

I want the birds to build their nest in a safe place. Soon the nest would have eggs and it would be too late. I'm trying to save these nestlings!

Of course the birds didn't understand. They fluttered about scolding us all day, but in a few days they were happily building in the backyard apple tree high enough so as not to have to worry about the cats.

"Father" help me to remember that I am safe in your love and care even when we must use tough love.

Because loving makes us vulnerable, we must be willing to take the risk of being hurt if we truly love.

§

LOVE IS ALWAYS WORTH THE PRICE!

Some people talk about "finding God" as if "he" could ever get lost!

The only answer to our loneliness is love . . . . not our finding someone to love us but our surrendering to the "God" who has always loved us with an everlasting love.

WHO IS GOD?

God is not a person such as we are:

"He" is a spirit being of love and light.
"He" IS Love. Made up totally of love.
"His" love for us has no beginning and no end.
Total love emanates from "Him"!
"He" exists in unapproachable light . . ."His Holiness".

§

"He" loves us so much that the bible tells us "He" collects our tears in a bottle.

§

"God" runs my life better than I do. I must remember to stay out of "His" way.

JESUS NEVER TAKES "HIS" EYES OFF YOU

"He" tells us, "Eyes have not seen nor ears have heard what "God" has prepared for those who love "Him". (1 Corinthians 2:9)

§

Age does not protect you from love, but love, to some extent, protects you from age.

§

"He" will always be there for you because "He" loves you as if you were the only one in the world.

"Father", you tell us that when we are weak, you are strong. Even if we forget you, "Lord", you are faithful and will never forget us."

§

"He" listens to my prayers for help. I will call to "Him" for help as long as I live. (Psalms 116:1-2)

"GOD" KNOWS YOU WELL

"God" knew you even then, before you came to be
For "He" fashioned only one of you, unique, as you
could be.
"He" watched you, oh so carefully, as you grew nice
and strong.
"His" eyes were on you every day through all your
rights and wrongs.
"He" watched you choose your lifelong mate
And nurtured it with care.
The children that "He" lent you were such a special pair.
"He" watched them leave and saw your tears.
You knew it had to be.
For they were only lent to you
And this "God" let you see.
"He" watches still your every move
Your pleasures and your pain.
Your age is catching up to you
Your life begins to wain.
But "Jesus" never leaves you.
"He" watches all you do.
"He" even loves your wrinkles and the gray hair
shining new.
"He'll" hold your hand and walk with you
Till life on earth is through.
Then "He'll" surely be there to smile and say
"I've been waiting just for you!"

Butterflies count not months but moments . . . . and yet have time enough.

§

Spend your life loving and lifting people up not putting them down.

§

Don't ever think that sending a gift or flowers substitutes for your presence.

§

Unless I can forgive, I cannot love!

§

You will never be asked to forgive someone else more than "God" has forgiven you.

"God" loves us even after "He's" seen us at our worst. That's forgiveness!

"Jesus Christ" has never failed to forgive anyone who honestly and sincerely asked for forgiveness.

A LITTLE LOVE GOES A LONG WAY

The church was having their annual tag sale the next day. The seniors club asked their members if they could arrange things on the tables the night before.

Everyone was doing their best distributing the items on the tables. Everyone, that is, but Marge, who was walking among the tables complaining and supervising. The ladies were getting upset with her. She moaned and complained about everything.

Ella tried to be patient with her, but even she was beginning to lose her patience.

Ella tried to be friendly but Marge always made a snide remark. Why was she so miserable? It seemed nobody knew.

Marge came to the senior club every day. They provided lunch for the seniors. She would always sit by herself looking kind of sad. The senior bus would take her back home.

One day, Marge missed the bus and Ella's son offered to take her home. She was hesitant, but she finally agreed.

As Bill pulled up at the address Marge gave him, he noticed what a dilapidated neighborhood she lived in.

There had been extra rolls and bread left over from lunch and Marge took a large bag home. Bill carried it up the two flights of stairs to her apartment. Marge grumbled all the way. She opened the door and thanked him quietly. He noticed it was only one room with a bed and an occasional chair. A small table sat by the window. He said goodbye and left.

Ella then knew why Marge always grabbed the best of the bread. She had almost nothing else. Marge always got their first for lunch. Ella knew it was probably because this was her only meal all day. Marge always wore the same clothes to the club. Could it be because this was all she had? Ella had seen some lovely sweaters come in for the tag sale. She would put them away and say she forgot to put them out. She knew Marge would grab them up.

Perhaps Marge felt like she didn't belong.

Ella decided to overlook Marge's attitude and try to be a good friend. It took her a good month, but Marge finally decided she needed a friend and opened her heart. Things had been pretty rough on Marge. Her husband was dead, they had no children who could help her and her small monthly check just wouldn't stretch far enough. Ella's heart broke just listening to her.

Little by little Marge's attitude began to change. She stopped complaining and even began to laugh a little.

Ella made sure that anything left over from lunch was put aside for Marge. She even invited Margie (Ella liked Margie better and so did Marge) over for Christmas dinner so Margie would not be spending Christmas alone. She even went to church with them. As it turned out, Margie became the most devoted friend Ella had ever had.

Margie's quality of life really blossomed because she no longer felt alone.

"GOD" CAN MAKE A WAY WHERE WE THINK THERE IS NONE!

LOVE IS FORGIVENESS

My mom had a disagreement with her brother when they were younger. They hadn't talked to each other in years. She often wanted to call and tell him she was sorry, she intended someday to just drop in and see him.

When she read he had died of cancer, she went to his wake. When she went to kiss her sister-in-law, she told my mom. "He always hoped you would come." My mom had let her pride rule her thoughts.

Do you need to put aside your pride and ask forgiveness before it is too late? Sometimes a simple phone call is enough to change a person's life . . . . and yours.

Let "God" do the mending!

You can feel blessed if you still have time to mend broken relationships before these people pass away. After "Jesus" takes them home, it will be too late.

§

The heart is like a parachute. It works only when you open it.

§

Hearts are like wings when they are opened with love.

§

Are you coping with yesterday's failures? Are things that happened in your past troubling you?

So many of us wish we had done things differently. These things only weigh us down and tend to take even more energy from us.

I don't know about anyone else, but I need all the energy I can get. Why not give these problems to "Jesus". He knows about them anyway!

LILACS WERE ONLY AN EXCUSE

I was in the kitchen warming soup for lunch when the doorbell rang. Visitors were mighty scarce lately, so the doorbell startled me. I opened the door to see a gray-haired lady holding a huge bunch of lilacs. She introduced herself as Lucy. She said she had moved in with her daughter next door and thought I might like some of her lilacs.

I thanked her as I invited her in. I could tell by her big wide smile and her air of enthusiasm that I liked her already. Oh! How I needed a friend!

After putting the lilacs in water, adding another can of soup for lunch and chatting about our families, we both realized that we had a lot in common.

It seemed like she had been here only an hour, but when we checked, it has been four hours. We had talked about so many things. We found ourselves laughing together. What a wonderful afternoon we had.

Only last week, I had been telling "Jesus" that I've been kind of lonely lately.

"He" never fails! Not only did "He" put her in my path but she likes so many things that I like too!

Chapter 5

So . . . What's In A Cup And Saucer?

Our grandchildren will not remember us for our laugh lines or wrinkles. They won't remember us for our spic and span house, but they will remember us for the cookies we bake with them, the nights they stayed overnight and you let them stay up late, the popcorn you popped together, your big wide smile when you opened the door for them and the things you told them about their family from years ago. These are the things that are so vivid to them. You are their loving Grandma. To them you are the most wonderful person they know.

What we leave in our children and grandchildren is far more important than what we leave to them

Listening to our grandchildren is a large part of our showing love for them.

When we age with dignity, we attract the admiration and the affection from our families and our grandchildren.

What a thrill it is when one of them says to you, "When I get old, I want to be just like you."

As we think back on the years of our lives, we can remember so many of the miracles which we know were not just coincidences. Perhaps we need to share these miracles with our grandkids. They need to see and know the wonders "God" can perform.

GRANDPARENTS

Their favorite gesture is open arms.
Their favorite words are "I love you, honey".
They never look for mistakes or failures.
They forgive very easily.
They love to listen when you want to talk.
They forget all else when you arrive for you are the center of their lives.

They let you know that you are more important than any possession they have. Remember when you accidentally broke Grandma's expensive vase? She just laughed and said it was a hunk of junk anyway. This made you feel so much better.

WHAT'S IN A TEACUP?

I have a lovely collection of cups and saucers. Each one is unique. Every one of them is a different colorful pattern.

This morning I decided to take them off the kitchen shelf and wash them. As I filled up the sink with water, I began lifting them gently into the sink. Just then the doorbell rang! It jolted me, and I dropped the cup I had in my hand onto another cup in the sink. Both of them broke, and one of them was my favorite.

I answered the doorbell and there stood my granddaughter. She had a short day in school, and her mom dropped her off for a surprise visit.

Of course, I forgot all about the cups. They were only material things. I had too many of them anyway!

Please, "Lord", let me always put people first. The people we love are always so much more important than any of our "things".

I will miss those cups, but I will live just fine without them, I'm sure.

Grandchildren are so much fun, we should have them first.

§

Grandmas hold our tiny hands for just a little while, but they hold our hearts forever.

§

A grandparent is old on the outside but young on the inside.

§

A grandma pretends she doesn't know you on Halloween

§

A grandma will accept calls from anywhere . . . . even if you call collect.

§

Grandchildren follow examples not instructions!

§

You should never say no to a gift from a child.

§

When playing games with your grandchildren, always let them win.

§

Grandchildren need a lot more smiles and hugs than lectures and instructions

§

Sometimes when we are living on a fixed income, we find it difficult to buy our grandchildren the things we'd like to. Personal experience has proven that spending time with them is far more meaningful than spending money on them.

- An afternoon at the beach collecting shells and letting them make sand castles.
- A picnic at a park and a Frisbee game
- A trip to the zoo to see the new baby tigers
- A trip to the ice cream parlor

The gifts of life, fun, and love outweigh anything mere money could buy them

§

A grandparents eyes see miracles where others see messes.

§

There are two places where a child is welcomed, church and grandma's house.

AN ATTITUDE OF GRATITUDE

The soul that complains can find comfort in nothing. The soul that gives thanks can find comfort in everything.

Spend more time counting your blessings . . . not airing your complaints.

God's gifts seldom come to us wrapped in lovely paper and topped with big fat bows. Sometimes they arrive in a new paperboy who brings your newspaper right up to your front door. Sometimes they come in the form of a neighbor who asks if you need anything as she goes food shopping. Gifts also come in the form of Mr. Behar, your neighbor who repaired your mailbox that was knocked over by the plows over the winter. He also takes your garbage cans out every Tuesday night. Look around, I'll bet you'll see so many gifts without pretty paper bows. These are the very best gifts sent down from the "Father".

As long as we are on the subjects of gifts, I remember some of the lovely gifts I used to receive for birthdays, anniversaries, etc.

I remember boxes of elegant chocolates, terrific smelling bath products, lovely silk nightgowns.

Now I get gifts like warm itchy sweaters, watering cans for my plants, four tubes of Bengay, a super warm flannel nightgown.

I'm thankful for all of them, but I think you get the picture here. Well, anyway, I absolutely love the flannel nightgown.

THANKFUL FOR ANOTHER DAY

Another day; it's raining I see
So I think I'll make a cup of tea
I'll sit and plan what I have to do
I'm thankful to be inside and cozy too

When life seems hard and I'm feeling low,
I sit with "His Word" for "He" wants me to know that
I am "His" child and "He" loves me so.

§

An attitude of gratitude gives us grit and gusto for living. Life is far too short to dwell on what I do not have, instead, I focus on what I do have.

A GET WELL GIFT

Winter waved its weary goodbye as we sprang into spring. It had been a very bad winter for me. I had been ill and going from doctor to doctor. I finally found one that could help me. After a number of tests, he diagnosed a severely stressful colon syndrome. It would take time with much rest and medication to get it under control.

One spring morning, as I rinsed off my dishes, I noticed a busy bird fluttering outside my window. As the morning went on, I discovered that two little birds were making their nests in the high hanging planter outside my kitchen window. As the days went by, it seemed like the mother bird flew busily back and forth.

One morning I looked out and saw three little yellow beaks sticking up. I could hear their noisy little squeaking. I enjoyed ever bit of it!

Everyday I watched eagerly as the father bird scavenged for food. He would give it to the mother bird and she would chew it up small to feed her babies. It was wonderful to see.

I watched as they grew. One day I saw one of the little birds leap to the rim of the nest. It started to fly but was very unsteady. It flew to the gutters above the nest and then flew off. The second little bird left the next day, but the third baby was having trouble. He climbed up on the rim of the nest three times but always went back into the nest. On the fourth try, the father bird flew into the nest. He actually took his beak and pushed the baby out of the nest. He dropped a few feet in the air and then flew up and out into the world. I laugh every time I remember this.

As I gave this some thought, it suddenly occurred to me that God had given me a precious gift with these little birds. I was so thrilled watching them that it took my mind off of myself as I became stronger. God knew I needed this nest. How I thanked "Him".

And every spring I scatter some soft cut up yarn to help soften all the new little nests.

By the way, this was God's one-time gift for me. The birds never returned to the planter again.

"Thank you, "Father". "How wonderful you are!"

DO YOU HATE TO ASK FOR HELP?

As we grow older, we must accept the help that people offer us. Of course we hate to give up our independence.

Dollie was always used to taking her winter curtains down and putting her light summer ones up by herself. She had been able to do this by herself last year, but since then there has been a weakness in both knees and it hurt too much to stand on the footstool.

When her daughter brought her groceries that evening, Dollie asked if she would have a few minutes to put up the curtains.

How surprised Dollie was when Gina grabbed her, kissed her and thanked her for letting her do this.

Gee, Mom, I wish you'd let me do a few things to help you, you always say "don't worry about it" but it makes me feel so good to know I'm helping you.

Dollie thanked her, and for the first time, she realized that perhaps they both received a blessing. "God" certainly has a great sense of humor.

"God's" promises are treasures waiting to be discovered.

§

Our difficulties in life are to make us better not bitter.

§

The gem cannot be polished without friction, nor a man perfected without trials.

 *Chapter 6*

An Attitude Of Gratitude

Help me, oh Lord to see your face
In the flowers, the grass and trees.
I often pray for your presence, Lord
Till I realize it's in all I see
Your love is so vivid around me.
For all that there is you've made.
Your sky with the moon and a trillion stars
Not diamonds or gold would I trade
Your whisper of love in the wind I hear
Is another promise your love is near
The whippoorwill singing in the backyard tree
Is a very special gift to me
I love you, my child, "He" seems to say
My presence is with you every day.

❧Chapter 7

He Never Takes "His" Eyes Off Of You

Are you finding it rough in your tiny apartment? Or maybe you're still living in the family home . . . . alone? Do you sometimes get depressed? Well, don't despair. No one ever said it would be easy living those "golden years" alone.

You can be the one the grandchildren love to visit. Your attitude can affect everyone in your family.

It's not easy to be enthusiastic, especially when those snap, crackly and pop knees of yours are aching, but people are less likely to want to be with someone who moans about everything than someone who greets you with a smile and says "Oh, I'm so glad you came".

No one is perfect, my best friend has a saying "no home is a church". I always laugh because this is so true.

Even though families and friends sometimes let us down (and) how this hurts. You have a friend who will never leave you and "He" loves to solve our problems because "He" loves us so much. So why not "Try God".

"Jesus" is waiting to guide you out. To restore your hope, and to give you peace.

Then shalt thou call and the "Lord" shall answer, thou shalt cry and "He" shall say, "Here I am"
(Isaiah 58)

§

I will instruct thee and show thee in the way which though shalt go. I will guide thee with mine eye.
(Psalm 32:8)

§

In all thy ways acknowledge "Him" and "He" shall direct they paths
(Proverbs 3:6)

DO NOT BELIEVE YOU WALK ALONE
BECAUSE YOU NEVER DO
HOLD OUT YOUR HAND AND YOU WILL FIND
THAT "GOD" IS THERE FOR YOU.

Help me never to doubt you. Hear me "Lord", for your mercies are new everyday.
"Father", I thank you for the certain knowledge that when I call upon you, you will answer me.

I love visiting the seashore. It takes my mind to a different world. I pick up a few special shells to take home. This never fails to perk me up for the rest of my day. The warm sand in between my toes feels so good.

§

My wish for you throughout the years that pass so quickly by
I wish you always laugh lots more than you will ever cry

§

A well-known psychiatrist recommends ten big belly laughs a day:

At my age I've seen it all!
At my age I've heard it all!
At my age I've done it all!
I just can't remember it all!

ONLY TWO WILL DO

Jenny emptied the can of turkey into Fluff's bowl. This was her favorite cat food, but Fluff didn't seem hungry. When Jenny sat down in her recliner, fluff climbed up in her lap and sighed, Somehow, Jenny thought, Fluff wasn't like her loveable self tonight. She petted her lovingly.

When her TV program was over, she gently lifted Fluff off her lap and went to bed. Fluff usually climbed in with her during the night.

In the morning, she was surprised that Fluff wasn't in bed with her. She went into the kitchen to make coffee and she noticed that Fluff's bowl was still full of food. Something was wrong. She found her beloved Fluff curled up gently in a corner.

Her son buried Fluff in a lovely afghan Jenny had made. She could not think of Fluff not being with her, so her son buried her underneath the laurel bushes in the yard.

A month went by and how she missed her Fluffy". She always gave back double the love that Jenny gave her. Her Fluff had been a dear friend for so long.

DOUBLE TROUBLE

One afternoon as she brought a bag of garbage out to her larger pail in the back yard, she heard some tiny squeaky noises in her garden. There sat two little kittens, probably four or five weeks old. Had someone dropped them off? Did they stray away from a mother cat who didn't have a home?

It was cold out, so she went for a box and took them inside. One was a tabby with a white tummy and four white paws. The smaller one was calico with a beautiful blend of colors. They were the noisiest little things. She fed them oatmeal with milk. They ate every drop of it. How funny they looked with oatmeal all over their paws and faces. She cleaned them up and made them a warm bed in the box with one of her old warm sweaters. They curled up together in one of the corners of the box.

Jenny called all of her neighbors to see if they knew the mother cat, but no one had seen her.

She decided to fatten them up for a few weeks. Then she would put an ad in the paper and a sign on the fence.

They did everything together. They were inseparable. They ate, slept, played and even fought together. They were using the litter box now, so she let them run free in the house.

They chewed up her new slippers together, they climbed her delicate lace curtains together. They unrolled a whole roll of toilet paper together. Jenny knew she had grown to love them. She put the ad in the paper and the sign on the fence.

The paper boy wanted the little tabby, but couldn't take both of them. Jenny said "no", the kittens went together or not at all!"

Mr. Jackson, the town barber wanted the calico one but his wife said only one. Jenny said "No" again.

As she watched them playing together, she wondered why she was giving them away. They always make her laugh. They both climbed into her lap at night. She couldn't even remember the last time she felt lonely. Those two little kittens occupied so much of her time.

Sometimes "Jesus" gives us a double whammy when we pray to "Him" because "He" loves to give "His" children over and above all they ask.

§

The wisest people we know are not the ones with the most years in their lives, but the most life in their years.
"Max Lucado"

§

We, ourselves, realize that these senior moments seem to turn up more often than we'd like, but keeping humor in our lives keeps us younger and happier.

§

Humility is not thinking less of ourselves, it is thinking of yourself less. It is thinking more of others. Humble people are so focused on serving others they don't have time to think only of themselves.

§

When we finally go to "Him" in our desperations, it is then that we realize we should have gone to "Him" in the first place.

Chapter 8

It Takes Guts To Leave The Ruts

Before I even get out of bed, I have a visitor who is there to greet me every morning. Arthuritis is his name. I always serve him up with a generous helping from my old friend, Ben Gay.

I can spend the day in bed thinking of the difficulty I have with the parts of my body that no longer work well, or I can get out of bed and be thankful for the ones that do.

NO ONE LIKES TO HURT

This morning isn't good, "Lord".
I'm sore as I can be.
Arthritis really has me down.
I'm tired of being me.

I'd really like to stay in bed,
and sleep the day away.
But there are things that I must do,
So, I reach for my Ben Gay.

Once I'm up and moving
I'll have my cup of tea.
Then, on the counter is my "Celebrex"

Waiting there for me.
And now I feel much better, and
can do what I must do.
Please let me spend my day, "Lord",
in loving and serving you.

When life with all its problems
renders you depressed,
seek out your "Lord", your "Savior" for "He" is
peace and rest.

When your problems overwhelm you,
"He'll" hold you in "His" palm
You'll feel "His" kindness and "His" love
as "He" restores your calm.

"Jesus" tells us in the bible to <u>fear not</u>.
As a matter of fact, "He" tells us this 365 times.

§

"Fear thou not" for I am with thee. Be not dismayed, for I am thy "God".
I will strengthen thee; yea, I will help thee, Yea I will uphold thee, with the right hand of my righteousness.
(Isaiah 41:10)

§

Planting is such fun, even churning over the tough winter dirt. I do it with pleasure, for I must remember that every flower that ever bloomed had to push its way through an awful lot of dirt to get there.

§

And so it is with us. Sometimes we have had to go through some difficult experiences to build our character. "God" goes through them with us!

§

No one can live on a continuous emotional high. For to live life; we must also live with valleys as well as mountaintops

§

We experience God's strength in the strain of our struggle.

§

I can do all things through "Christ" who gives me strength.
(2 Corinthians 12:9)

OUR OLDER CITIZENS ARE SUCH TREASURES

Our older people contain so much knowledge. Years ago, they were treasured for their wisdom. This is not so today, sometimes they are ignored and even forgotten.

Older men and women have such interesting stories to tell. They have lived through so many experiences.

My mom lived through the war when food was rationed. She told me of recipes made from what little they had. They were delicious as well as thrifty. I still use so many of them.

The men tell stories of the wars, of losing friends that were standing right next to them in the battles. They tell us how much was given to keep our country free. They tell us that Freedom is anything but free!

Our seniors should not be looked on as inconveniences. We should consider them as true treasures. They are a very welcome balance to our young-crazy world.

THERE ARE BLESSING TOO!

Sometimes when it's damp or raining, that dampness gets into these old bones. It's then that I count my blessings as my wonderful mailman delivers my mail right to my door.

A NEW DOOR OPENS EVERY DAY

I cannot understand, "Lord"
Why you let me live
With all the pain and hurt I have
I don't have much to give

But, by your grace you've let me see
That you, "Lord" hold the key
A new door opens everyday
That lies ahead of me

So, Thank you "Lord" for this extra time
I know there's so much more
We'll walk together "hand in hand"
Till we reach that special door

Your last chapter in life can be the very best. Your final debut can be your very best. Sometimes we need to be unselfish around the ones we love, and that's not easy. We can do this if we have a vision of heaven and of Christ waiting for us.

GO AWAY, LONELINESS

I smile when I really don't want to.
I push myself when I'm down.
No one needs know when I'm lonely.
Why burden them with a frown.
I do what I can so I'm useful.
I keep myself going all day.
Loneliness creeps in so slowly.
But, I'll continue to push it away.

TAKE TIME TO APPLAUD YOURSELF

By the grace of "God" you are somebody Marvelous:

- You are a truly remarkable creation.
- You have been given incredible endurance.
- You can accomplish almost anything once you set your mind to it.
- You can be a channel of "God's" Joy.
- You always try to have a positive attitude.
- Others admire your helpful ways.

§

I'll keep a smile upon my face
There's much I want to do
Whatever "God" has in store for me
To "Him" I will be true

§

There is only one thing I have to do right now . . . . I am going to make the most of today

§

With attitudes like this you will not only be beautiful on the inside but on the outside too!

§

I'm trying, therefore, I am a success.
No matter how my day turns out, I'm getting the badge
of courage for trying.

DON'T LEAVE A BAD IMPRESSION

A quarrelsome, grouchy old women created an awful ruckus as she stepped off the bus. She threw an insult at the driver and criticized a few of the passengers harshly.

Just before he closed the door, he called out to her. "Lady, you left something behind."

She stopped, turned around and grouchily asked, "Oh what".

"A terrible impression of yourself", said the driver as he closed the door.

LET'S LAUGH

I don't suffer from insanity, I enjoy every bit of it.

§

You're just jealous because the voices only talk to me.

§

I'm not a complete idiot . . . . some parts are missing.

§

God must love stupid people. "He" made so many of them.

§

Consciousness: that annoying time between naps.

FLOWERS DO NOT MAKE A SALAD

Jean could never wait for spring to come. She loved every minute she spent in her garden. She spent hours cleaning, weeding and planting. She never regretted her time spent there. It was her pride and joy. All the neighbors envied Jean's green thumb. She would give arms of flowers to all of them when they bloomed.

The exciting hours she spent in her garden made her days so much more interesting.

How often she thanked her "Lord" for the ability to be able to still get down on her knees to do the weeding. She laughed, as she said "Lord, the worst part is getting up again, could you please work on this for me?"

Maybe next year I'll plant a vegetable garden too. It's pretty hard to make a salad out of flowers even as beautiful as they are.

The bible tells us:
For God has not given us a spirit of fear, but of power and of love and a sound mind.
(2 Timothy 1:7)

Chapter 9

God Is On The Night Shift Too!

If fear and worry test your faith, and anxiousness prevails, remember "God" is in control, and "He" will never fail!

GOD NEVER SLEEPS

Lettie rubbed her eyes. She went into the kitchen for water. She needed to stay awake (or so she thought). It was 2am and she should have been in bed long ago. She was afraid to go to sleep because three homes within a four block radius of her home had been broken into during the last two weeks.

She had been awake for almost three days now, and she was absolutely miserable.

She finally put the problem in "God's hands, for "He" never sleeps and "He" is always on the night shift!

"God" is our refuge and our strength, a very present help in time of trouble.
(Psalm 46:1)

Fear is powerless unless you feed into it.

Many of our senior citizens live alone. Any noise or knock on the door scares them. Even a phone call when no one answers on the other end scares them.

"God" understands their fears, and "He" has so much to say in "His" word to be of comfort.

Do not be afraid or discouraged for the "Lord" is the one who goes before you. He will never fail you or forsake you.
(Deuteronomy 31:8)

BE STILL AND KNOW THAT I AM "GOD"!
(Psalm 46:10)

TWO DARK STRANGERS

Ed was a little worried! His supply of food was very low. His daughter usually kept him well stocked, but she has been ill with the flu for over a week now. He had no milk left, no bread for a sandwich, not even an egg in the refrigerator.

He decided to get his cane and walk the two blocks to the store.

He had no trouble getting there and finding the things he needed. Even the bags of groceries were light and he had no trouble holding it even with his cane in the other hand.

As he left the store, he noticed two young men leaning against the storefront smoking and laughing. One of them said "Hi Pops". Ed said "hello" to be polite.

As he started walking home, he thought he heard the two boys laughing a short way off. Just as he rounded the corner to his street, he looked back, he was right. They were following him. Ed was weak. He knew he would be easy prey, for he couldn't run and it was getting dark. Being alone he feared the worse. The men were getting closer now.

Ed looked up to his "Heavenly Father" and asked "Him" to help.

The men were almost upon him when he reached the few steps going up to his apartment. All of a sudden Mr. Hayden from the apartment above him rushed out to help him. Mr. Hayden gently scolded him for not letting him and his wife do his shopping for him.

The two men grimaced and continue on down the street. Ed thanked Mr. Hayden and told him how scared he was. Mr. Hayden had gone to the window to shut it when he saw Ed coming around the corner. He had not even seen the men following Ed.

Ed put his groceries away and then he gratefully sank down in his recliner and thanked "God" for "His" help and "His" mercy.

This was not the first time "God" had intervened in Ed's life, nor would it be the last!

Have you ever been so afraid that you were at the point of losing your ability to deal with the circumstances around you? You hear others talking but nothing seems to register. You realize you are out of control!

These are the times when you will know whether you really trust "God" or not. "He" is in control of your life. "He" tells you to cast your cares on him, because "He" is the one who cares for you.
No matter how small the problem is, if it concerns you, then it concerns "Him".

UNFAMILIAR SOUNDS

It had been a rainy evening which had erupted into unusually high winds accompanied by thunder and lightening. She hated it even worse since her husband died. Being alone in a thunderstorm was just about the scariest thing Anna could imagine.

There was an unfamiliar banging on the front porch. She could not place the sound, and she was worried.

Her children had tried to convince her to move into the large first floor bedroom, but she decided to stay in the room she and Bob were in for forty six years.

The unfamiliar banging was scaring her, but she was afraid to go downstairs. She hated living alone. She was up all night worrying, but by the time morning came, she had convinced herself to move downstairs. She would have better control of the house this way . . . and her nerves.

After breakfast she decided to go outside and see what might have been banging in the storm. To her surprise, a shutter had broken off it's hinges and was banging in the wind. Thank "God" for sons. He always wanted to help her, and now there would be a few things to do.

She was also going to take a trip to the city dog pound that afternoon. She needed a dog, a good watch dog as well as a loving companion.

Anna just remembered, she must take down her wall hanging when the room was moved. It was what kept her from being paralyzed with fear all last evening. It read:

"FEAR NOT, FOR I AM WITH YOU ALWAYS'

The "Lord" is near to all that call upon "Him". The "Lord" is close to the brokenhearted and saves those whose spirits are crushed.
(Psalm 38:21-22)

§

There are approximately 773,692 words in the bible, but the word "worry" is not in "God's" vocabulary. Should it be in yours?

§

The most effective sleeping pill is . . . . peace of mind.

§

You never need fear of going to bed at night because . . ."God" is on the nightshift too!

§

True faith sees "God" in the darkness as well as in the light!

§

More than half of all people over sixty five complain of insomnia. Sometimes it can be a spiritual opportunity. Being alone with "God" in the middle of the night. Wow!

§

We can come to "Him" with unconfessed sins or it may be simply opening our hearts and being alone with "Him".

§

THE PEARL

It is difficult for us to understand why suffering and sometimes pain can result in a persons becoming compassionate and understanding.

The origin of the creation of the pearl might somewhat explain this. A pearl is formed when a grain of sand enters an oyster causing an irritable wound. Resources within the oyster rush to the injured area which finally results in a lustrous pearl. Something beautiful is created that would have been impossible without the wound.

❧*Chapter 10*

Laughter Enriches Our World

I live in my own little world, but it's okay they all know me here.

§

My friends are always giving me new beauty secrets to try, but when they suggested putting hemorrhoid treatment on my face to tighten the skin, that's when I drew the line!

§

The human being is the only creature on our planet that has been given the gift of humor.

§

It's the best when you can laugh with a friend because you both think the same things are funny.

WHEN WE LOOK BETTER, WE FEEL BETTER

The mailman came to the front door, he was quiet and gave me a funny look as he asked me to sign the registered letter he was delivering. I signed it, and he left quickly.

Twenty minutes later as I passed by my mirror in the bedroom, I realized what I looked like

My nightgown (which was my oldest and most comfortable one) was hanging out at the neck. It was all raveled and coming apart. My robe was old too. It's not that I didn't have newer ones, but these were so comfortable.

My hair (which I hadn't combed yet), still had the two curlers hanging in the front. I must have scared my poor mailman half to death.

Our "Lord" demands that we should always do what is right. We must be careful to be properly dressed each day.

Not only when others see us, but we will feel better when we look better. My poor mailman! I sure hope he has a sense of humor.

I hung up the phone and said goodbye. I said I was glad to be of help. My friend, Fay had called me from the grocery store. She locked the keys in her car . . . again! I called the locksmith and met him and Fay at the store.

This was not an isolated incident. I was beginning to worry about her. In the last few weeks she had:

- Locked herself out of the house (I have an extra key she gave me)
- Lost the gas cap after filling up her car (did she put it on tight enough?)
- Left two bags of groceries at the market (we went back to get them)
- Promised to pick up her grandchildren at school, only to forget about it (her daughter is still angry with her).
- Forgot her son's birthday
- Lost her checkbook (it is still missing)

Fay is seventy-seven years old and I am seriously worried that she might be "Losing it" so to speak, I try to help her all I can.

One day I decided that I needed a few new pairs of slacks. I went to Walmart. I chose 2 pairs and went to the dressing room. They fit fine so I proceeded out of the dressing room to the check—out counter.

As I was walking to the register, I noticed people pointing and one little boy pointed and said "Look mommy", and started laughing.

His mother quietly came over to me and told me that my skirt was tucked up in back and stuck in the waist of my pantyhose. I was mortified and thanked her for telling me. (half the store could have told me) From now on I will never wonder about Fay's senior moments for I'm having a few of my own.

§

"We need a good laugh"

§

Older people should not eat health foods. They need all the preservatives they can get.

§

One of the best things about being old is, you will probably be among the first hostages to be released.

§

Age doesn't matter . . . . unless you're a cheese!

§

An archeologist is the best friend a woman can have. The older she gets, the more he's interested in her.

Now I lay me down to sleep
I pray the Lord my shape to keep
Please no wrinkles, please no bags
And please lift my rear before it sags

Please no age spots, please no gray
As for my tummy, please take it away

§

No way I'm this fat. The dry cleaner must have shrunk
my pants.

§

Why aren't there more bathing suits with skirts?

§

There's a slot machine in Las Vegas with a sign on it
that says, "in case of an atomic attack, hide under this
machine. It's never been hit yet!"

❧Chapter 11

Nearer Heaven's Gates

Sooner or later every bar of gold must pass through the fire and, sooner or later, we will all pass from life to death. It is not the finest part of our lives, but it is a very real part of life.

§

"Jesus" makes us a promise, and "He" keeps all of "His" promises. "I" will come back and take you to be with me. "He" promises to take you home. "He" would not let anyone else do this. "He" may send pastors to teach you, angels to guard you, doctors to heal you, but "He" himself wants the job of bringing you home to be with him for eternity. "Max Lucado"

§

"God" tells us that no one lives a day more or a day less than "God" intends.

§

All the days planned for me were written in your book before I was one day old.
(Psalm 139:16)

§

"God" never said the journey of life would be easy. But, "He" did say arrival would be worthwhile. "Max Lucado"

§

For a Christian, heaven is spelled
H-O-M-E!

§

Dearest "Lord",
Grant me knowledge to know that "He" who notices when a sparrow falls to the ground, took note of your loss with "His" tears. "He" cares when "His" children grieve.

§

"He" healeth the broken hearted and bindeth up their wounds.
(Psalm 73:24)

§

A GENTLE ANSWER

As she sat on her porch, her heart ached for her son who had just gone home to the "Lord".

She thought, "Children shouldn't die before their parents do."

She screamed at "God", "where were you when my son died?"

"God" answered her so very gently, "the same place I was when mine died."

It is always so difficult to realize that "He" gave us life and "He" has the right to take it back whenever "He" wishes.

§

If you believe, you will know that death is just the beginning of life. To live eighty years is just the drop of a pin compared to eternity.

§

When you lay your head down for the last time, you will find that your life will be only beginning!

§

Even though we walk through dark valleys, "Jesus" will be there walking right beside us. "He" will be there at your bedside, "He" will cry with your loved ones as they say goodbye. And . . . . "He" will be there to smile and take your hand and lovingly bring you home where you will be with "Him" forever!

Billy Graham, a famous preacher says:
I'm convinced that when we die, we immediately enter the presence of the "Lord". At some future time, we will be given new bodies similar to the body "Jesus" had after "His" resurrection. But in the meantime, our souls are with the "Lord" and we are conscious of "His" presence.

§

So many of us wonder if making peace and coming to God at the end of our lives will be too late. They wonder if "He" will forgive them. Proof that "He" will is in the forgiveness "Jesus" gave the thief as he hung on the cross. It is never too late to be forgiven. He loves all of us and he wants no one to perish.

§

The resurrection shows the limitlessness of God's reliability.

§

THE HIGHEST PLACE IS ALWAYS AT THE FOOT OF HIS CROSS

HE LOVED THEM TO THE END

A minister was boarding at a farmhouse. The farmer himself was not a Christian but his wife was. For some time the minister had been waiting for an opportunity to make plain to this farmer the real meaning of "Christ's" sacrifice on Calvary.

Early one morning, the farmer called the minister and said "I want to show you something in the chicken house. As they entered the coop, they saw a hen sitting in her nest with a brood of little chicks peeping out from under her wings.

"Touch the hen," the farmer said. As the minister put forth his hand to touch the hen, he noticed that she was dead. She was cold and had been dead for hours. "Look at the wound in her head", said the farmer. During the night a weasel came and drained her body of the last ounce of blood, but she never moved from the spot in her nest for fear her little ones might suffer harm. The minister saw his opportunity to draw a homely comparison that would be meaningful to his friend. As they walked slowly back to the farmhouse, the pastor surprised his friend by using the incident they had just witnessed as an illustration of the love of "Christ", of whom the scriptures tell us that having loved "his" own, "He" loved them to the very end!

"Jesus" knew that on that first Good Friday, "He" could at any moment, come down from the cross but "He" also knew that there were millions whom "He" had come to save. For them, "He" was prepared to die! Praise God that included you and me! Having loved "His "own, He loved us to the very end!

When English patriot Sir William Russell went to the scaffold in 1683, he took his watch out of his pocket and handed it to the physician who had attended him. "Would you kindly take my timepiece" he asked, "I will have no use for it now, I am dealing with eternity."

WITH THESE HANDS

When not much of anything else of me works well, these hands hold me up, they lay me down and continue to fold in prayer.

Then someday "He" will take my hands to lead me home.

And . . . . with these hands, I will touch the face of my precious "Jesus"!

§

LIFE'S GREATEST WORRY

Nothing makes us more uneasy than the thought of what happens to us after we die.

Ask most people if they are going to heaven and they'll say "I hope so". Or maybe, "if I'm good enough". If they're honest, they'll tell you that the thought of death terrifies them.

Well, I'm here to tell you that you can absolutely know without a doubt that when you die, you will go to "Jesus" and the paradise "He" has for you!

Your requirements for heaven have already been met for you, "Jesus" paid your debt for sin when "He" died on the cross for you. The penalty of sin is death you know.

"Jesus" rose from the dead proving that His father accepted "Jesus's" sacrifice on the cross.

Our sins are forgiven!

"God" is satisfied with "Jesus's" perfect sacrifice!

We can't buy our way into heaven. Nothing we could do (no matter how good it was) could get us in there.

All "He" asks us to do is put our trust in "Jesus", tell "Him" you believe "He" suffered for your sins and that they are forgotten and you are forgiven.

"Jesus" said, "most assuredly, "I say to you, he who believes in me has everlasting life."
(John 6:47)

"Jesus" also said, "There are many rooms in my father's house." "I would not tell you this if it were not true." I am going there to prepare a place for you. "I" will come back and take you to be with me so that you may be where "I" am."
(John 14:23)

"Jesus" never lies! It is impossible for "him" to lie. Does this sound incredibly easy? Does it ask very little of us? Yes, "God" made it easy. "He" loves you and "He" wants you to be with Him.

Easy? It is anything but easy. "Jesus" suffered more than any man ever suffered, and it was for you and me!!

"Jesus" said, "Because I live, you will live also!!" (John 14:19)

"God's" word tells us: Eyes have not seen nor ears have heard the wonders God has provided for those who love "Him".

"Jesus" is at the door of your heart. Why not open it and let "Him" in? And . . . . when your candle finally flickers, he'll be there to open "His" gates for you FOREVER!!!

Now that you have been told, you need to make the decision only you can make. No one else can do it for you!

UNTOLD millions are perishing because they were . . . UNTOLD!

God sent Jesus down on a rescue mission. "He" died so you might live!

What Jesus actually did was pay your debt! AND . . . . your debt is PAID IN FULL!

SALVATION IS A GIFT THAT ANYONE CAN OPEN!!

WANT TO GIVE YOUR LIFE TO CHRIST?
HERE'S HOW

Your life is getting shorter
Your time on earth is too.
So . . . . if you want "Jesus" in your life
This prayer is just for you.

"He's" always ready to listen to a repentant heart that's true.
For "He" wants no one to perish.
"He" died to prove that to you.

So go to "Him" in prayer
You'll find it easy to start.
For "He's" been there all this time
Waiting at the door of your heart.

PRAYER

"Lord Jesus",

I believe that you died on the cross for my sins. Please forgive me. I believe you rose from the dead. "I now receive you as my savior". I want to be with you forever. Thank you "Jesus". Amen

§

The one who comes to me I will by no means cast out.
(John 6:37)

MY HEART HAS HEARD YOU SAY,

"COME AND TALK WITH ME, OH MY PEOPLE"

AND MY HEART RESPONDS,

"LORD, I AM COMING" (Psalm 27:8)